Mama, Why Am I Homeschooled?

Written by Jacy Ruwe

Illustrated by Elin Johnson

@CuriousCoonhoundBooks & @ElinJohnsonArt

 /CuriousCoonhoundBooks & /ElinJohnsonArt

 JacyRuweAuthor & ElinJohnsonArt

This book is dedicated
to the tired mama
who's pretty sure
she's screwing it all up.
Grace changes *everything*.

Curious Coonhound

BOOKS

Mama,
why am I homeschooled?

Because snuggling up in a cozy chair
with a good storybook
is the most wonderful way to enjoy
a cold and rainy Tuesday morning.

Mama,
why am I homeschooled?

Because picking apples at the local orchard
and lugging our heaping baskets to the scale
is the most delightful way to accomplish
some physical exercise.

Mama,
why am I homeschooled?

Because swinging on the front porch
with a mug of warm cider
is the most wonderful way to take course
the ever-changing seasons.

Mama,
why am I homeschooled?

Because baking and decorating
sugar cookies with Daddy
is the most delightful way to master
those pesky sight words.

Mama,
why am I homeschooled?

Because doing random acts of kindness
for unsuspecting folks in town
is the most wonderful way to celebrate
an unrushed spring break.

Mama,
why am I homeschooled?

Because pausing to pen
an "I love you" letter to Auntie
just because we were thinking of her
is the most delightful way to polish
important writing and grammar skills.

Mama,
why am I homeschooled?

Because sewing felt dolls and superheroes
for the patients at the children's hospital
is the most wonderful way to cultivate
a neat handicraft.

Mama,
why am I homeschooled?

Because adding sketches
to our nature journals
while we hike along the forest trail
is the most delightful way to explore
our creative inner-artists.

Mama,
why am I homeschooled?

Because shopping for the ingredients
for our favorite meal
and racing each other to add up the total
is the most wonderful way to brush up
on tricky math facts.

Mama,
why am I homeschooled?

Because meeting up with friends at co-op
to train our new robots to dance
is the most delightful way to hone in
on the latest coding techniques.

Mama,
why am I homeschooled?

Because putting on a recital
for the residents of the assisted living center
is the most wonderful way to rehearse
an audience-captivating performance.

Mama,
why am I homeschooled?

Because jumping in the car
for an impromptu visit with far-away family
is the most delightful way to grasp
how to read and follow a road map.

Mama,
why am I homeschooled?

Because tending and harvesting
our backyard vegetable garden
is the most wonderful way to learn
about the recurrent cycles of life.

Mama,
why am I homeschooled?

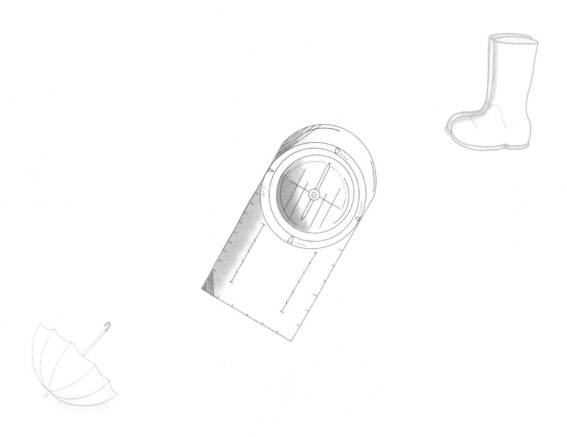

Because crafting our own covered wagon
and trekking it across the golden prairie
is the most delightful way to role-play
our honored pioneer heritage.

Mama, why am I homeschooled?

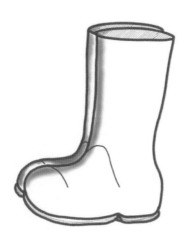

Because staying up past bedtime
to lay on the grassy hill
and discover new constellations
is the most wonderful way to conclude
a lovely school day.

Mama, why am I homeschooled?

Because spending each day learning
alongside my dearest ones
is the most delightful way to cherish
the precious time I have with you.

Mama,

I'm so glad
I'm homeschooled.

Jacy Ruwe is a teacher turned homeschooling mom and professional aunt. She has a BA in Elementary Education with an endorsement in Early Childhood Education and has taught in both public and private schools. Jacy lives on a small homestead in Nebraska with her husband, Andy, and their herd of free-range kids and pets. When she's not schooling or writing, she enjoys studying Christian apologetics and reading on the front porch. *Mama, Why Am I Homeschooled?* is her first children's book.

Elin Johnson was born and raised in the Swedish archipelago. She majored in art and drama in high school and studied graphic design at a Swedish university. Elin later met her American husband, Andrew, and moved to the U.S. in 2010. They now reside together in Rochester, Minnesota with their three boys and cat. Elin stays busy painting custom work for clients, designing labels for a local brewery, and illustrating children's books. She is an avid birdwatcher, nature lover, and novice gardener. *Mama, Why Am I Homeschooled?* is the second book she has illustrated.

Made Beautiful By: _____

Printed in Great Britain
by Amazon